MIL MI-26

BY QUINN M. ARNOLD

CREATIVE EDUCATION • CREATIVE PAPERBACKS

Published by Creative Education and Creative Paperbacks
P.O. Box 227, Mankato, Minnesota 56002
Creative Education and Creative Paperbacks are imprints
of The Creative Company
www.thecreativecompany.us

Design by The Design Lab
Production by Chelsey Luther
Art direction by Rita Marshall
Printed in the United States of America

Photographs by Corbis (Marina Lystseva/ITAR-TASS Photo,
ANATOLY MALTSEV/epa, ILYA NAYMUSHIN/X01151/Reuters,
Dai Tianfang/Xinhua Press), Dreamstime (Maria Berglind,
Meoita), Flickr (Dmitry Terekhov), Newscom (LAURENT
GILLIERON/EPA), Shutterstock (Artyom Anikeev, InsectWorld)

Library of Congress Cataloging-in-Publication Data
Arnold, Quinn M.
Mil Mi-26 / by Quinn M. Arnold.
p. cm. — (Now that's big!)
Includes bibliographical references and index.
Summary: A high-interest introduction to the size, speed, and
purpose of the world's largest helicopter, including a brief history
and what the future holds for the Mil Mi-26.

ISBN 978-1-60818-714-0 (hardcover)
ISBN 978-1-62832-310-8 (pbk)
ISBN 978-1-56660-750-6 (eBook)
1. Mi-26 (Helicopter)—Juvenile literature. 2. Helicopters—Juvenile
literature.

TL716.A75 2016
623.74/65—dc23   2015045209

CCSS: RI.1.1, 2, 3, 4, 5, 6, 7; RI.2.1, 2, 4, 5, 6, 7, 10; RF.1.1, 3, 4;
RF.2.3, 4

First Edition HC 9 8 7 6 5 4 3 2 1
First Edition PBK 9 8 7 6 5 4 3 2 1

TABLE OF CONTENTS

4

What helicopter can carry more than 100 people? The Mil Mi-26 can lift the biggest loads of any helicopter. Many countries use Mi-26s.

Each Mil Mi-26 is flown by a five-person crew.

This helicopter is 26.6 feet (8.1 m) tall. It is as long as three buses. It has eight rotor blades. Each blade is 52.5 feet (16 m) long! There are five smaller blades on the tail.

Two military tanks can fit inside an Mi-26 cargo hold.

More than 300 Mi-26s have been built. The Soviet Union made the first one to move heavy equipment. Cargo comes in through the rear door. In 1982, an Mi-26 took 22.9 tons (20.8 t) of cargo more than 1.2 miles (2 km) high!

The Mi-26 uses its six big wheels to land.

The Mi-26 flies 158
to 183 miles (255-295
km) per hour. It has
two powerful engines.
If one engine stops
working, it can still
land safely.

An aircraft must be empty of fuel before the Mi-26 moves it.

Mi-26s have picked up helicopters and airplanes that have crashed or broken down. They use a sling to lift the broken aircraft. In 1999, an Mi-26 moved a 25.4-ton (23 t) ice block. Inside the ice was a woolly mammoth!

1000

In 2007, an Mi-26 carried a boat over mountains in Switzerland.

The Mi-26 helps people, too. It delivers food and other supplies. It flies in bad weather. It flies to places where there is fighting.

Some firefighting Mi-26s can carry fire retardant in the cargo hold.

Some Mi-26s are made
to give medical help.
They have rooms
for doctors to work.
Others can carry
thousands of gallons of
water. They help put
out fires.

A loaded Mi-26 can go 497 miles (800 km) before it has to stop to refuel.

China and Russia
are building a bigger
helicopter together.
But Mil Mi-26s are
still flying. They will
keep helping people
for a long time.

2016

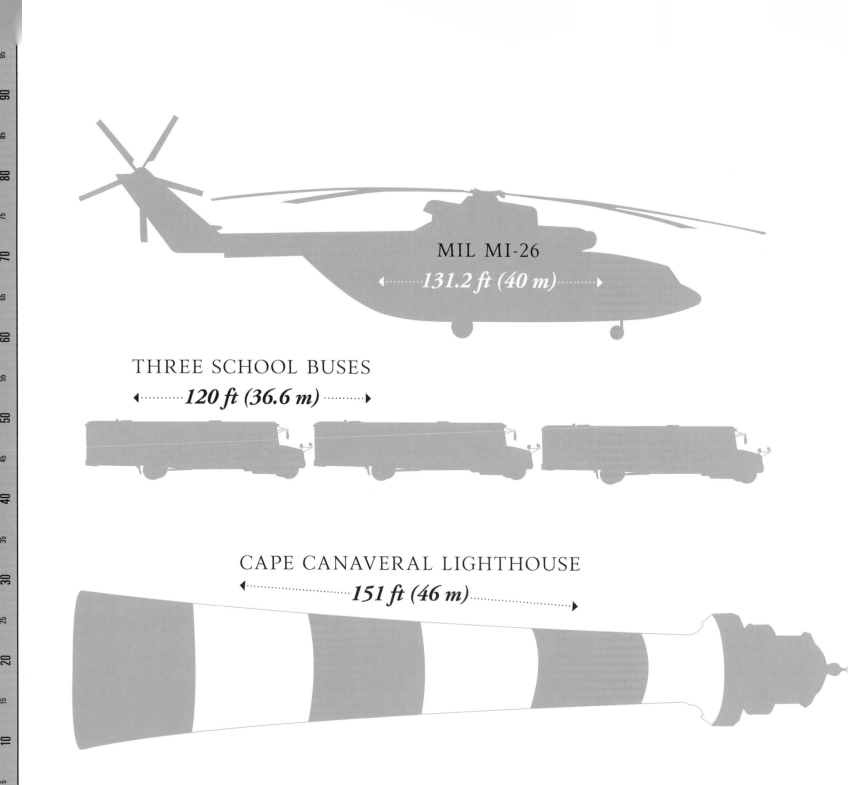

MIL MI-26
131.2 ft (40 m)

THREE SCHOOL BUSES
120 ft (36.6 m)

CAPE CANAVERAL LIGHTHOUSE
151 ft (46 m)

FIRST-GRADER
3.6 ft (1.1 m)

SEMITRAILER TRUCK
70 ft (21.3 m)

BLUE WHALE
100 ft (30.5 m)

BOEING 737 MAX 8
138.2 ft (42.1 m)

GLOSSARY

cargo—*objects carried by an aircraft*

engines—*machines that use fuel to create movement*

rotor blades—*the long blades that spin around to lift a helicopter into the air*

sling—*a device used to carry cargo below a helicopter*

woolly mammoth—*a large, hairy animal that lived in cold northern regions; most died out by 10,000 years ago*

READ MORE

Confalone, Nick, and Chelsea Confalone. *Helicopters*.
New York: Grosset & Dunlap, 2015.

Riggs, Kate. *Helicopters*.
Mankato, Minn.: Creative Education, 2016.

WEBSITES

Flight Lesson Plans
http://www.sciencekids.co.nz/lessonplans/flight.html
Explore the web page to learn about flight, and then design and build your own paper helicopter.

Helicopter Facts & History
http://www.chetours.com/our-fleet/helicopter-facts-history/
From Leonardo da Vinci's sketches to the first working helicopter, learn more about the history of helicopters.

Note: Every effort has been made to ensure that the websites listed above are suitable for children, that they have educational value, and that they contain no inappropriate material. However, because of the nature of the Internet, it is impossible to guarantee that these sites will remain active indefinitely or that their contents will not be altered.

24